Poems to
Take on
Holiday

'10

1

Other books by Susie Gibbs

Poems to Annoy Your Parents
Poems to Freak Out Your Teachers
Poems to Make Your Friends Laugh
Poems to Make Your Friends Scream

Poems to Take on Holiday

packed by Susie Gibbs

illustrated by Jess Mikhail

OXFORD

UNIVERSITY PRESS

OXFORD

UNIVERSITY PRESS

Great Clarendon Street, Oxford OX2 6DP

Oxford University Press is a department of the University of Oxford.
It furthers the University's objective of excellence in research, scholarship,
and education by publishing worldwide in

Oxford New York

Auckland Bangkok Buenos Aires Cape Town
Chennai Dar es Salaam Delhi Hong Kong Istanbul Karachi
Kolkata Kuala Lumpur Madrid Melbourne Mexico City Mumbai
Nairobi São Paulo Shanghai Taipei Tokyo Toronto

Oxford is a registered trade mark of Oxford University Press
in the UK and in certain other countries

British Library Cataloguing in Publication Data
Data available

ISBN 0 19 275391 6

1 3 5 7 9 10 8 6 4 2

Printed in Great Britain
by Cox & Wyman Ltd, Reading, Berkshire

Contents

When You're There

Home Again

Time to Set Off

The Pessimist's Holiday

Read this one before you go anywhere

It will probably start with the taxi being late,
we just can't find the tickets or
a passport's out of date.
If we make it to the airport all flights will be delayed,
long queues at the check-in desk,
tempers getting frayed.
The hotel will be half built and the pool a brownish-grey
and we're sure to all get sunburnt
on the first or second day.
The noise of the disco will keep us awake at night
and drilling will start prompt at 6
on the local building site.
Food and water dodgy, the air-conditioning broken,
then we'll realize it's been several days
since Mum and Dad have spoken.
Coming home we set off in the middle of the night,
allowing extra time for
the latest airline strike.
If we happen to land safely, our luggage gone to Rome,
then probably we'll all agree
we should have stayed at home.

Jane Saddler

Check List

Poem to be said when sitting in the car, ready to leave home

Mum: Have we got everything, darling?

Dad: Of course we have, dear:
All our cases
travellers' cheques . . .
   medicines and swimming things
   tickets, spare cash
   insurance stuff
   driving licence
   suncreams too.

Mum: Off we go!
Wave goodbye . . .
plants and catfood
   all is well.

Daughter:	Have we got the rubber dinghy?
Dad:	On the roof rack nice and firm oars and rudder lifebelts, rope.
Son:	What about the sunglasses?
Mum:	In my handbag three spare pairs books and papers tissues, pens.
Dad:	Well done, everybody.

* * *   * * *   * * *

Customs man: Passports, sir?

Peter Dixon

No Passport

Poem to be said on discovering you've forgotten your passport

Oh!
No!!

Gerard Benson

Luggage Lament

Poem to be read very loudly at the luggage carousel

Lumbering luggage around
is a nightmare, the very worst
holiday trauma of all.
It gets lost,
it gets scattered,
broken and battered,
and always weighs more
than it should or it ought.

It breaks all Mum's fingernails,
crushes Dad's toes,
falls on the baby,
blocks all the rows;
and getting a drink
is like climbing Mount Everest
with suitcases, rucksacks,
and bags to get round.

So I'm starting a protest.
Down with all luggage!
Look at it this way,
however it's viewed
it would be far less hassle
and ten times more fun
if we all took our hols
in the nude.

Patricia Leighton

Seeking the Elusive Trolley

Poem to be read in a David Attenborough voice

Here in the baggage reclaim hall,
If you wait very patiently,
You may just be lucky enough to see,
The shy and reclusive baggage trolley.
In this, once its normal habitat,
It has now become a rare sight,
Driven out by the hordes of people
Pushing it, until its wheels wear out.
Now you may more readily find lone trolleys
Lurking shyly around corners and in
Dark areas under stairwells.
Their normal gathering places are now
The deep dark of the car park
Or warmth of the Booking Hall
Where they stand more chance
Of being left in peace.

Pat Gadsby

I Spy

Observation at the airport

I spy with my little eye,
Hundreds of people all waiting to fly.
But don't get excited: no one knows when—
The baggage handlers are on strike again.

Marcus Parry

Bags Bags Bags Bags Bags Bags Bags

The airport luggage carousel song

Where's me bag bag bag bag bag?
Where's me bag bag bag bag bag?
At the big carousel
It's the song that I yell at the
Bags bags bags bags bags bags bags
At the bags

In the line line line line line
Which is mine mine mine mine mine?
At the big carousel
It's the song that I yell at the
Bags bags bags bags bags bags bags
At the bags

Here it comes comes comes comes comes
Near me mum's mum's mum's mum's mum's
At the big carousel
It's the song that I yell at the
Bags bags bags bags bags bags bags
At the bags

Catch it now now now now now
Don't care how how how how how
At the big carousel
It's the song that I yell at the
Bags bags bags bags bags bags bags
At the bags

Here it is is is is is
And I've . . . missed missed missed missed missed
At the big carousel
It's the song that I yell at the
Bags bags bags bags bags bags bags
At the bags

There it goes goes goes goes goes
With me clothes clothes clothes clothes clothes
At the big carousel
It's the song that I yell at the
Bags bags bags bags bags bags bags
At the bags

Where's me bag bag bag bag bag?
Where's me bag bag bag bag bag?
At the big carousel
It's the song that I yell at the
Bags bags bags bags bags bags bags
At the bags

Adam Smith

Holiday

Poem to read quietly to oneself as things get worse

Mum is crying her eyes out
And Dad is going insane
Because someone has left a suitcase
On the London—Glasgow train.

And Dad says it has to be Mum's fault
So Mum starts blaming me
So naturally I blame Ollie
And Ollie blames Emily.

Then Emily starts having hysterics
And Mum starts feeling unwell
And Ollie starts throwing up
On the airport carousel.

Then Dad can't find the tickets
But I know he searches in vain
Because I know those tickets are travelling
In the case on the Glasgow train.

And I think of our poor lost suitcase
Slumped glumly on the rack
Travelling up to Glasgow
And then travelling all the way back.

Or dumped in some Lost Luggage Office
With a jumble of other lost things
Umbrellas and coats and sets of false teeth
Handbags and wedding rings.

But oh, little suitcase, of one thing I'm sure
Wherever you happen to be
I'm certain you must be having
A happier holiday than me.

Gareth Owen

In the Airport Waiting Lounge

Poem to keep people's spirits up

Look on the bright side,
we're here in the dry
and I'm sure that tomorrow
we'll be up in the sky.
You'll find if you read
it passes the time
or have a nice sing-song—
that isn't a crime.
It's a bit of a bore
with the pilots on strike
but I'll do a tap dance
for you if you like.
I've been learning for weeks.
Here I go, tra la la.
You may see me in movies
when I'm a star.
Well, you're all looking grumpy
and I've run out of puff.
Perhaps I was not
entertaining enough.
The pilots can't help it—
they want lots more cash.
The happier they are
the less likely to crash.

Let's play I spy,
something starting with P.
You won't need a holiday
now you've got me.
So look on the bright side
for I too, you know,
am stuck at the airport
with nowhere to go.

Marian Swinger

wait and wait Again

Poem to read when nothing seems to be happening

Wait at the bus stop.
Wait in the rain.
Wait on the journey to
Wait for the train.
Wait while it takes you to
Wait for your plane.
Wait at the flight gate.
Wait there in vain.
Wait and wait and wait and wait
And wait and wait again.

Wait at the help desk.
Wait to complain.
Wait while the staff there
Wait to explain.
Wait with your passport.
Wait but remain.
Wait till the waiting
Drives you insane.
Wait and wait and wait and wait
And wait and wait again.

Wait on the tarmac.
Wait on the plane.
Wait while the plane's weight
Takes the flight lane.
Wait for a cloud-break.
Wait to see terrain.
Wait while you circle.
Wait to land again.
Wait and wait and wait and wait
And wait and wait again.

Wait in the gangway
Waiting to deplane.
Wait for your suitcase.
Waiting is a pain.
Wait with a headache.
Wait while your brain
Waits to see if waiting
Triggers your migraine.
Wait and wait and wait and wait
And wait and wait again.

Nick Toczek

Postcard from South America

A useful poem to glance at before boarding your plane

Venice!

City of calm, clear canals,
of graceful, gliding gondolas,
of peaceful, pleasant piazzas,
of canal-side, candle-lit cafés,
of shimmering, shining ships,
of beautiful bridges and buildings,
of ancient, elegant art,
of fantasy, fable, and fame.

Yes, Venice would have been nice.
If only we'd checked the boarding gate twice!
Venezuela's not quite the same.

Kate Williams

Venezuela — Venezuela

(20·08·04)

venezuela

Venezuela!

To Gran

Gran's big house

Somewhere

SS1 PO2

Take-off

Prayer to whisper when you're already in your seat

Dear God, help the pilot to remember what to do.
Please, God, kindly make the engines work OK,
the nose lift
and the runway long enough . . .
And when you have done all that,
please sweep up the electric storms and turbulence
and sort out the air traffic control people
   (who don't speak our language).
Also, please—
in the unlikely event
of
landing in the sea,
please may the little light on my life jacket
shine properly
and can the man from Australia
with 'Lifeguard' on his shirt
be in my dinghy?
You will find me, God,
in seat 13A—near the wing.
That's all—
except the landing—which I hope you will sort out
satisfactorily.
There was something else.
  Oh yeah—
    thanks!

Peter Dixon

Air Cares

Poem to read to the nervous passenger sitting beside you in the plane

How long does it take to plummet thirty
   thousand feet?
Have you checked your life preserver's
   underneath your seat?

Will the safety belt hold if we hurtle
   through the skies?
Who'll be left to tell the tale if everybody
   dies?

Will we get some warning to adopt the
    brace position?
Are all the engines safe, and in a good
    enough condition?

Have they filled the hold up tight with everybody's
    cases,
Or has our luggage been dispersed and sent to
    different places?

Oh no, I think we're moving. Is the door
    quite firmly shut?
What happens if the flight computer fails and goes
    kaput?

They're serving up prawn cocktail and a dodgy
    chicken stew.
What if we're all poisoned, and the captain, and
    the crew?

I've taken half a travel pill, but still I might
    be sick,
So if I yell 'The bag, the bag!' please pass it
    to me quick.

To tell the truth, I'm feeling fine, but you've
    turned rather green.
I'll make an educated guess that flying's
    not your scene.

Alison Chisholm

Turbulent Travel

Poem for the pilot of this very bouncy plane

If we survive this nightmare flight
And feel our feet on firmer ground
I might be quivering with fright
But you won't hear me make a sound.

I'll race off home without a care
I'll jump about, forget my fear
I'll be alive to breathe fresh air
Not trapped in this tin tube up here.

Just turbulence, I hear you smile
Above the straining engine's roar
But we've just fallen half a mile
Straight towards the ocean's floor.

This plane of yours flies like a brick
Plummeting from cloud to cloud
Mum feels ill and Dad's been sick
Panic's spreading through the crowd.

The cabin crew are looking pale
My stomach fizzes, my ears pop
Please land us safely, do not fail
Just make this awful dropping stop.

With your computers and those lights
Flashing on that space-age gizmo
Surely you can make your flights
Less bouncy than a giant yo-yo?

The coast of Spain is where we've been
All hot and warm, really sunny
But in this airborne trampoline
Life really isn't all that funny.

At last I feel the wheels touch down
The wings stayed on, there's the sprawl
Of blazing lights that's London Town.
What d'you mean, not there at all?

What's that? We've landed back in Spain?
The air's too thin, the storm's too rough?
Tomorrow we will try again?
You're joking, pal, we've had enough.

We won't be flying home with you
We'll all kick up an awful fuss
I'll tell you this, I'll tell you true
We are going home by bus.

David Harmer

In the Sky

Poem for the air stewardess

How high in the sky are we, please, stewardess?
Nine or ten miles up. That is *my* guess.
What have you got on that big breakfast trolley?
A strawberry ice or a raspberry lolly?
How does the plane stay up in the air?
If an engine drops off, have you a spare?
Have you some parachutes stored, just in case?
If we go any higher, will we reach space?
Do you get bored up in the sky?
You *look* very bored. Was that a sigh?
Look, out of the window, a huge UFO!
Ha! Caught you there. I was joking, you know.
Could I try on your cute little hat
or help push the trolley? Did you see that?
A lady's been sick right there in the aisle.
You'll have to mop up. That'll take you a while.
I'm glad I'm not you. It's a horrible smell.
In fact, stewardess, help. I've been sick as well.

Marian Swinger

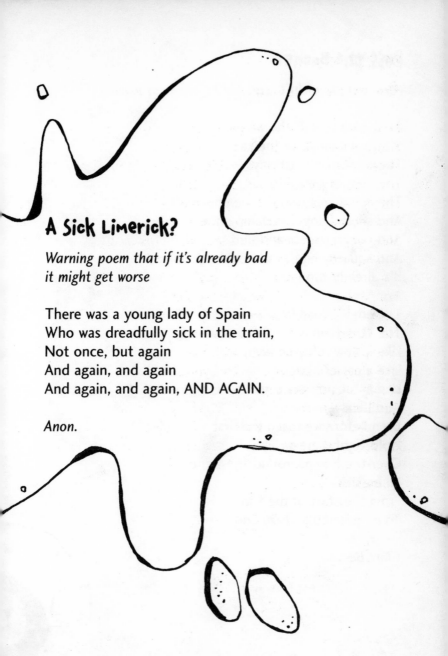

A Sick Limerick?

*Warning poem that if it's already bad
it might get worse*

There was a young lady of Spain
Who was dreadfully sick in the train,
Not once, but again
And again, and again
And again, and again, AND AGAIN.

Anon.

Pass the Bucket

Poem you shouldn't read just before a car journey

As soon as I sniff the warm,
Stuffy, inside air of the car,
The whiff of old ashtrays,
The gust of petrol fumes,
The musty mixture of stale chocolate
And snuffly dog and damp shoes
And cough sweets and fluff
And squashy egg sandwiches,
It's already too late.

The engine rumbles,
The street lurches up and down
Like a slow roller coaster,
Like a camel's back,
Like an unstoppable sea,
And I know,
Even before we reach the first
Hold-tight, here-we-go,
Over-the-bumps, round-the-bend,
I'll be sick
From the start of the trip
To its miserable, dizzy end.

Clare Bevan

Travel Sickness

Poem to read while clutching a paper bag

Sick in the taxi
Sick on the train
Sick in the airport
Sick on the plane
Sick on the coach
And sick again.
Sick six times
From here to Spain.

Nick Toczek

Feeling Ferry Funny

Poem for the ferry

Sailing away on a belly-flop ferry,
watching a porthole as though it's a telly,
hypnotic waves swilling round on the screen,
swishing and a-swoshing, and turning me green,
churning up my stomach till it's full of froth.
Feel ferry funny and I want to get off.

Gina Douthwaite

Travel Game

Poem to liven up the landscape

Sitting on buses
or in the back seats of cars
I pass the time
by imagining a huge scythe
jutting out like a wing.
As we speed along,
this curved blade slices through
all that it meets.
Telegraph poles tumble,
trees become stumps,
hedgerows are trimmed
to the length of new grass.
Nothing is too tough
for my imaginary scythe.
It hacks through hills,
slides through steel
and breaks through bricks.
I see tower blocks become bungalows,
houses become huts
and mountains become molehills,
as hours are chopped down to minutes
and seconds are whittled away.

Steve Turner

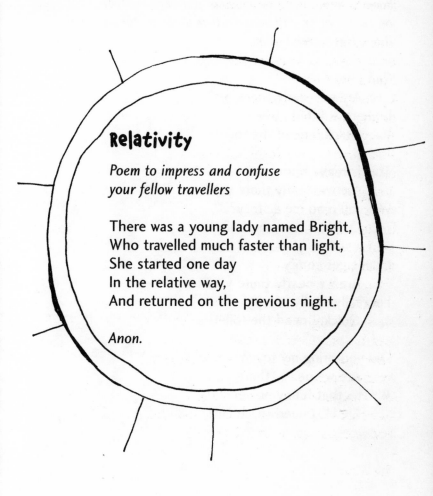

Relativity

*Poem to impress and confuse
your fellow travellers*

There was a young lady named Bright,
Who travelled much faster than light,
She started one day
In the relative way,
And returned on the previous night.

Anon.

Belt up in the Back!

Poem to read aloud on long car journeys—either on your own or with your brother or sister, taking it in turns to read a line

Can I have a sweet?
 Are we nearly there yet?
Is there anything to eat?
 Quick, I need the toilet!

This is really boring.
 Are we nearly there yet?
Will you read me a story?
 Quick, I need the toilet!

I can't get comfy.
 Are we nearly there yet?
I'm really, really hungry.
 Quick, I need the toilet!

Did you bring my toys?
 Are we nearly there yet?
What's that funny noise?
 Quick, I need the toilet!

Can we have some music?
    Are we nearly there yet?
I think I feel car-sick.
    Quick, I need the toilet!

I'm really, really thirsty.
    Are we nearly there yet?
I'm just about bursting.
    Quick, I need the toilet!

Health Warning:
Repeated out-loud readings of this poem can drive the
grown-ups in the front crackers—and the car right off
the road.

David Horner

List of Car Songs your Parents Ought to Know

Sing them as loudly as you dare!

There's a Hole in my Bucket
If You're Happy
A Sailor Went to Sea
She'll Be Coming Round the Mountain
Clementine
My Old Man's a Dustman
The Drunken Sailor
Scarborough Fair
This Old Man
Pop Goes the Weasel
The Quartermaster's Stores
Frère Jacques
Michael Finnegan
Oranges and Lemons
The Skye Boat Song

A Trip to Morrow

Poem to be read in almost any travel situation

I started on a journey just about a week ago
For the little town of Morrow in the State of Ohio.
I never was a traveller and really didn't know
That Morrow had been ridiculed a century or so.
I went down to the depot for my ticket and applied
For tips regarding Morrow, interviewed the station guide.
Said I, 'My friend, I want to go to Morrow and return
Not later than tomorrow, for I haven't time to burn.'

Said he to me, 'Now let me see, if I have heard you right,
You want to go to Morrow and come back tomorrow night,
You should have gone to Morrow yesterday and back today,
For if you started yesterday to Morrow, don't you see,
You should have got to Morrow and returned today at three.
The train that started yesterday, now understand me right,
Today it gets to Morrow and returns tomorrow night.

'Now if you start to Morrow, you will surely land
Tomorrow into Morrow, not today you understand,
For the train today to Morrow, if the schedule is right
Will get you into Morrow by about tomorrow night.'
Said I, 'I guess you know it all, but kindly let me say,
How can I go to Morrow if I leave the town today?'
Said he, 'You cannot go to Morrow any more today,
For the train that goes to Morrow is a mile upon its way.'

Anon.

ways to Pass the Time

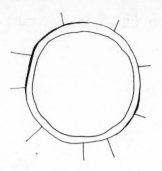

How to Reach the Sun . . . on a Piece of Paper

Something to fill the time

Take a sheet of paper
and fold it,
and fold it again,
and again, and again.
By the 6th fold
it is 1 centimetre thick.

By the 11th fold
it will be 32 centimetres thick,
and by the 15th fold
—5 metres.

At the 20th fold
it measures 160 metres.
At the 24th fold,
—2.5 kilometres
and by fold 30
is 160 kilometres high.

At the 35th fold
—5000 kilometres.
At the 43rd fold
it will reach to the moon.

And by fold 52
will stretch from here
    to the sun!
Take a sheet of paper.
Go on.
    Try it!

Wes Magee

The Sea

An endless song to while away long journeys

Pools prink plip
Ripples ring rocks
Surf sings softly
Fat foam flecks
White waves whip
Breakers beat boulders
Wind wildly whistles
Waves whack wallop
Wind wildly whistles
Breakers beat boulders
White waves whip
Fat foam flecks
Surf sings softly
Ripples ring rocks
Pools prink plip

Kevin McCann

She Sells Seashells

For chanting in spare moments

She sells seashells on the sea shore;
The shells that she sells are seashells I'm sure.
So if she sells seashells on the sea shore,
I'm sure that the shells are sea-shore shells.

Anon.

The Surprising Number 37

Something else to fill the time

The number 37 has a special magic to it.
If you multiply 37 x 3, you get	111.
If you multiply 37 x 6, you get	222.
If you multiply 37 x 9, you get	333.
If you multiply 37 x 12, you get	444.
If you multiply 37 x 15, you get	555.
If you multiply 37 x 18, you get	666.
If you multiply 37 x 21, you get	777.
If you multiply 37 x 24, you get	888.
If you multiply 37 x 27, you get	999.

Anon.

Travel Books to Read on Holiday

List for adding to when you're bored

SCANDINAVIAN ADVENTURES BY VI KING

EXPLORING FRANCE BY NORMAN DEE

SCUBA DIVING for beginners BY CORAL REEF

Paris in the Springtime by April Day

EATING OUT IN GERMANY BY FRANK FURTER

INSIDE SERBIA BY BEL GRADE

ALPINE SKIING BY VAL D'ISERE

AN AUSTRALIAN CITY GUIDE BY MEL BOURNE

TROPICAL BEACH RESORTS BY SANDY COVES

TRIPS ROUND CHINATOWNS BY RICK SHAW

John Foster

when you're There

At the Bed and Breakfast

Poem not to say to the landlady

Dad says the room is smelly
And that the beds have bugs
He says the carpet's sticky
And the bathroom's full of slugs
He says the food is fatty
And there's grease all round the place
He says all this behind your back
But never to your face.

Paul Cookson

Fantastic Facts

Add your own

Farmers
In the Bahamas
Seldom wear pyjamas

Police
In Greece
Often keep geese

The rain
In Spain
Sometimes travels by train

Most people in Cuba
Know how to scuba
But nobody plays the tuba

The well-to-do
In Peru
Always wear blue

No one wears a tie
In Paraguay
(Don't ask me why)

In Japan
A man
Isn't expected to carry a fan

The staff in hotels
In the Seychelles
Like ringing bells

In Mauritius
The food is delicious
And quite nutritious

The moon
In Cameroon
Rises at noon.

John Irwin

53

Postcard

Poem that sums it up

Hotel incredible
Food inedible
Rain falling
Bedroom appalling
Cockroaches persistent
Pool non-existent
Service slack
Money back

Ian Larmont

Frozen

Putting on a brave face

There was a young man of Quebec
Who was frozen in snow to his neck,
When asked, 'Are you friz?'
He replied, 'Yes, I is,
But we don't call this cold in Quebec.'

Anon.

The Fly

Poem to read when there's a fly in your hotel room

Bzzz. Bzzz. Bzzz.

I want to sleep but it's here again.
The fly.
Its buzzing goes right through my brain.
Oh why?
It's swooping low above my nose.
I sigh.
It scares me and I think it knows.
Don't cry.
It lands right by me on the wall.
Close try.
It leaves me with no choice at all.
Goodbye!

Bzzz. Bzzz. Splat.

Liz Walker

Holiday weather

Poem to read at breakfast

I'm sorry to have to inform you,
The sun has been cancelled today.
Would customers dressed in bikinis,
Put their overcoats on straightaway.

You may wipe off sun-cream at your leisure,
Fling your old straw hat far out to sea,
Fold the deckchairs and tell the landlady
You'll be wanting lamb hotpot for tea.

Bank holidays aren't just for people,
The sun's worked non-stop since July,
Now he fancies a day with his feet up
So hurry indoors where it's dry.

Petonelle Archer

The Bug Chant

Poem you shouldn't read if you don't like creepy crawlies

Red bugs, bed bugs,
find them on your head bugs.

Green bugs, mean bugs,
lanky, long, and lean bugs.

Pink bugs, sink bugs,
swimming in your drink bugs.

Yellow bugs, mellow bugs,
lazy little fellow bugs.

White bugs, night bugs,
buzzing round the light bugs.

Black bugs, slack bugs,
climbing up your back bugs.

Blue bugs, goo bugs,
find them in your shoe bugs.

Thin bugs, fat bugs,
hiding in your hat bugs.

Big bugs, small bugs,
crawling on your wall bugs.

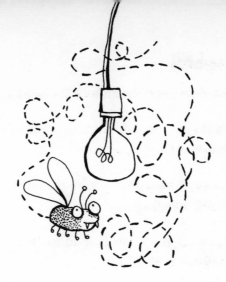

Smooth bugs, hairy bugs,
flying like a fairy bugs.

Garden bugs, house bugs,
lumpy little louse bugs.

Fierce bugs, tame bugs,
some without a name bugs.

Far bugs, near bugs,
'What's this over here?' bugs.

Whine bugs, drone bugs,
write some of your own bugs.

Bzzzzzzzzzzzzzzzzz . . .

Tony Mitton

On the Sunbeds

Poem to read when you're bored with sunbathing

Fidgety person: It's peaceful out here, don't you think?
Reading person: Mmm.

Fidgety person: What's that you're reading? Is it good?
Reading person: Mmm.

Fidgety person: D'you know how to fix these sunbeds?
Reading person: Mmm.

Fidgety person: I think I have it. D'you want some lotion?
Reading person: Mmm.

Fidgety person: I love this stuff, it smells of coconut.
Reading person: Mmm.

Fidgety person: Would you rub some on my back, please?
Reading person: Mmm.

Fidgety person: Are you sure that you don't want some?
Reading person: Mmm.

Fidgety person: Wow! It's really hot out here now!
Reading person: Mmm.

Fidgety person: Fantastic view, do take a look.
Reading person: Mmm.

Fidgety person: I'm so glad I brought this drink.
Reading person: Mmm.

Fidgety person: How 'bout a walk along the beach?
Reading person: Mmm.

Fidgety person: I think maybe I'll go and swim.
Reading person: Mmm.

Fidgety person: You'll be OK on your own then?

Reading person: Mmmmmmm.

Lucinda Jacob

Ouch!

Poem to read to your sister as she lies out in the sun

Shoulders red
Throbbing head
Peeling nose
Your back glows

Hot sore skin
Blistering
Sunburnt tum
Big white bum

Beverley Johnson

The Hunk

Poem to say to the lifeguard

You're strong and you are hunky
You're sexy and you're cute
You're masculine, good looking
In your tight bathing suit
Your muscles they are rippling
Your six pack, it is ace
Your chest is oiled and shiny
Like the smooth skin on your face
Your hair is long and bleached
Your eyes are deepest blue
I've just one thing to say . . .
My mum fancies you.

Paul Cookson

Ways to Get Into the Water

Poem to read to parents who suddenly jump out of their deckchairs and head for the pool

starfish
bellyflop
scissors jump
dive
sitting jump
knee-hug
whoosh! down the slide
backwards roly-poly

but if you're over 35 . . . use the steps!

Andrea Shavick

Make a Quick Guess

Poem to read when standing in the sea—if you dare!

My first is in swim but not in beneath,
My second's in hungry and also in teeth.
My third's in attack but isn't in blood,
My fourth's in rip but not in thud.
My fifth is in killer but isn't in cruel—
I can see you right now and I'm starting to drool.

Coral Rumble

Answer: Shark

Do Have a Nice Day at the Beach

A poem of advice for a younger brother or sister who's going for a day out by the sea when you're not

Although I'm ill and stuck indoors,
I hope you have a good day out.
You mustn't let my day spoil yours
As you all gaily play about.

For it's your first time by the sea,
So do enjoy the sand and sun,
But first hear this advice from me
To keep you safe while having fun.

The sun, though safe enough inland,
Is treacherous when at the coast,
So keep your coat on, by the strand,
Or else end up like crispy toast.

The sand: walk on it if you dare,
In shoes that have the thickest treads,
Or broken glass that's hidden there
Will quickly rip your feet to shreds.

The sea, although it seems quite calm,
Can swiftly sweep you far from shore.
The dolt who doubts its deadly harm,
And swims, will soon be seen no more.

Beware the lurking Jellyfish,
Its tentacles and lethal sting.
If slow and painful death's your wish,
The Jellyfish is just the thing.

And mind the Shallow-Paddler-Shark,
Which, searching round for things to eat
And finding you an easy mark,
Will neatly bite off both your feet.

Be wary of the Hairy Grampus
As it lumbers from the spray,
Attracted by the picnic hampers,
Crushing all things in its way.

And don't forget to watch the skies
In case the Red-Beaked Carrion Gull
Should swoop down and peck out your eyes
And rip your face right off your skull.

For many, many are the fools
Who've been on seaside holidays,
And failing to observe these rules,
All died in ghastly, grisly ways.

But though I'm stuck at home in bed,
I'm glad that you can go and play.
Just follow all these things I've said,
And have a happy, carefree day.

David Bateman

If You Go on Safari

A poem of advice

Don't pitch camp beneath coconut palms.
If you do, on your own head be it.

Though lions be large cats
do not try to stroke.

Do not swim with hippos and crocs.

Baboons and chimps may be our cousins
but draw the line at kissing.

Do not attempt to hug the python
or tickle piranhas like trout.

If you tell jokes to hyenas, remember
they will insist on the last laugh.

John C. Desmond

If You Should Meet a Crocodile

Another poem of advice

If you should meet a crocodile,
Don't take a stick and poke him;
Ignore the welcome in his smile,
Be careful not to stroke him.
For as he sleeps upon the Nile,
He thinner gets and thinner;
But whene'er you meet a crocodile
He's ready for his dinner.

Anon.

Faith

Poem to read to anyone about to swim in the sea

There was a young lady of Ryde,
Who was carried too far by the tide;
A man-eating shark
Said: 'How's this for a lark?
I knew that the Lord would provide.'

Anon.

Presence of Mind

Poem to read when considering an adventure holiday

When, with my little daughter Blanche,
I climbed the Alps, last summer,
I saw a dreadful avalanche
About to overcome her;
And, as it swept her down the slope,
I vaguely wondered whether
I should be wise to cut the rope
That held us twain together.

I must confess I'm glad I did,
But still I miss the child—poor kid!

Harry Graham

we're Not Eating . . .

Poem to read daily in the dining room

We're not having that paella stuff
With bits of fish and prawns.
We're not having them tortillas
We don't eat pancakes at home.
We're not eating any croissant things
They crumble to pieces when cut.
We're not eating calamare
It's like having snakes in your gut.
Just give us the chips and the burgers
Cold slush by the gallon instead
And give Dad his full fry-up breakfast
We're all used to being well-fed!

David Clayton

Unlucky You
or
why a Holiday in Blackpool is Better

Poem to read loudly and confidently

Travelling by car is much more fun
Than flying in an aeroplane.
Anyway, Mum gets airsick
And there's nothing to see when you're up in
   the clouds.

I'm glad we didn't go to Italy
Because I can't speak Italian
And Blackpool beach is underrated;
When it rains the glistening sands are beautiful.

In Italy, Alex says, the sound of the surf
Keeps you awake.
But we're not far from the beach.
It's only a ten-minute walk, if you run.

You don't see many dolphins from Blackpool beach
But, even better, we swam with the jellyfish.
We much prefer fish and chips.
Who wants to eat boring old spaghetti Bolognese,
   anyway?

I'm glad we went to Blackpool
Not to Italy, like my best mate Alex.
Mum says we mustn't tell him what a great time we had
He'll only be jealous.

Roger Stevens

Desperation—in Eight Languages

Poem for a sticky situation

English
Français
Nederlands
Deutsch
Italiano
Español
Svenska
Dansk

Excuse me,
Excusez-moi,
Neemt U mij niet kwalijk,
Entschuldigen Sie,
Mi scusi,
¡Perdóneme!
Förlät mig,
Undskyld,

I am feeling sick.
J'ai mal au coeur.
Ik ben misselijk.
Ich fühle mich krank.
Ho mal di cuore.
Tengo náuseas.
Jag känner mig flygsjuk.
Jeg føler mig dårlig.

Where are the toilets?
Où se trouvent les toilettes?
Waar is het toilet?
Wo sind die Toiletten?
Dov'è la toilette?
¿Dónde está el tocador?
Var är tvättrummet? Toiletten?
Hvor et toilettet?

I have diarrhoea.
J'ai la diarrhée.
Ik heb buikloop.
Ich habe Durchfall.
Ho la diarrea.
Tengo diarrea.
Jag har diarré.
Jeg har diarrhé.

I am in a great hurry.
Je suis très pressé.
Ik heb haast.
Ich habe es sehr eilig.
Io ho molta fretta.
Tengo mucha prisa.
Jag har mycket bråttom.
Jeg har meget travit.

Where are the toilets?
Où se trouvent les toilettes?
Waar is het toilet?
Wo sind die Toiletten?
Dov'è la toilette?
¿Dónde está el tocador?
Var är tvättrummet? Toiletten?
Hvor et toilettet?

I wish to make a complaint.
Je veux déposer plainte.
Ik wil een klacht indienen.
Ich möchte Anzeige erstellen.
Presentero denunzia.
Quiero hacer la denuncia.
Jag önskar göra anmälan.
Jeg vil klage over.

I want some toilet paper.
Je désire du papier hygiénique.
Hebt U toiletpapier.
Ich möchte Toilettenpapier.
Vorrei carta igienica.
Deseo papel higiénico.
Jag önskar toilettpapper.
Jeg vil gerne have toiletpapir.

Do you understand . . . ?
Comprenez vous . . . ?
Begrijpt U . . . ?
Verstehen Sie . . . ?
Comprende . . . ?
¿Comprende Vd . . . ?
Förstår Ni . . . ?
Forstår De . . . ?

Madeleine Bingham

A Curse on Thieves, Especially the One who Takes your Mum's Handbag

Poem I hope you won't have to use

May the paper money burst into flames and frizzle your
    eyebrows,
May the coins turn into cabbages in your pockets,
And may the credit cards ooze slug slime onto your
    hands for ever.

May Mum's clean hanky tie knots around your nose,
And her nail polish burn holes in your fingers and toes.
May the address book be possessed by a paper-spitting
    poltergeist,
May Mum's phone ring every time you try to go to
    sleep,
And may her lipstick write messages on your mirror.
    (You're nicked, sunshine.)

May my chocolate bar make you sick and pale,
And Dad's guide book lead you to the best jail. (Long
    stay welcome, BOOK NOW!)
May your dreams be as boring as embassy passport
    queues,
And may your nightmares be full of policemen.

Oh yeah.

Megan de Kantzow

The Loch Ness Monster's Song

Poem that can be understood in any language

Sssnnnwhuf ff fll?
Hnwhuffl hhnnwfl hnfl hfl?
Gdroblboblhobngbl gbl gl g g g g glbgl.
Drublhaflablhaflubhafgabhaflhafl fl fl—
gm grawwwww grf grawf awfgm graw gm.
Hovoplodok-doplodovok-plovodokot-doplodokosh?
Splgraw fok fok splgrafhatchgabrlgabrl fok splfok!
Zgra kra gka fok!
Grof grawff gahf?
Gombl mbl bl—
blm plm,
blm plm,
blm plm,
blp.

Edwin Morgan

Home
Again

Left Luggage

Poem to read on the journey home about all the luggage left behind in the hotel room

The chambermaid will love my mum's posh perfume,
it's nearly new and not much used up.
Dad's Speedo trunks we bought in the hotel shop
as his others were old and embarrassing and he'd
   forgotten to pack.

I couldn't care less about my sister's gear.
She's screaming and stamping she's left her hairdryer.
I think it's funny that her hair's a mess
and she's not wearing make-up—that also got left.

My baby brother is stinking the car out—
all the spare nappies are still in the hotel bathroom.
There are no motorway services in sight,
we're all choking to death and just about to faint.

I'm sure I haven't left a thing.
I'm feeling very happy and very smug.
I'm sure my Nikes are packed up in my bag.
My sister smiles nastily and tells me that they're not.

What! Stop! We're going back!

Lesley Marshall

The Journey Back

Poem to read before setting out for home in the hope that this year it might be different

Home from our holiday and someone says:
'What was it like,
did you have a good time?'
And I always say,
'It was great, it was fine,
apart from the journey back.'

Dad got stuck in traffic
as he tried out a new short cut.
Cars stretched on in the midday heat
while Dad kicked up an awful fuss,
honking and shouting at the car in front
till some chap who was built like a house
climbed out
and told Dad he'd better shut up!

Then Mum got talking and made Dad miss
the motorway turning he should have taken
and Dad had to drive an extra ten miles
just to turn around and come back.
Mum made it worse with her silly remark:
'Just a hiccup,' she said,
but Dad's face was black.

And then when we stopped for lunch
we were raided by squadrons of wasps
keen on snitching as much as they could
from our peaches and sticky buns.
Dad, of course, tried to play it cool,
'Sit still,' he said. 'Don't flap,
they won't hurt you . . . AAARGH!'

Mum had to drive after that,
Dad's finger was aching too much.
He kept on at Mum
not to crash the gears:
'Just give my ears a break,' she said,
'and let me get us home.'

Dad mumbled a bit then dozed
in the front, and I think it was
soon after that when I noticed
something was up with the car.
Every minute or so, it bucked
and went slow, but we covered
a couple more miles
till the engine cut.

Even Mum was angry now
and when Dad woke up and had a go
she gave him a piece of her mind.
'OK,' said Dad, 'we'll phone the AA,'
till he noticed his card was
out of date. What a day!

Six hours later the car was fixed
and Dad said, 'No way
are we going away next year.'

For once Mum said she agreed with him
but I tried to say that I thought
they were wrong, our holiday
had been really fun
apart from the journey back.

Brian Moses

what I Did in My Summer Holiday

Poem for the big post-holiday boast back at school

Oh, nothing much . . .

Climbed Everest one afternoon,
Went round the world in my balloon,
For England scored a last-kick winner,
Took Princess You-Know-Who out to dinner;
Outgunned Clint Eastwood in a Western,
Reached the South Pole—without a vest on!
Shot Niagara by canoe,
Cycled from here to Timbuctoo;
Became a pop-star, topped the charts,
Transplanted half a dozen hearts . . .

Nothing really supercool.
I'm thankful to be back at school.

Eric Finney

Holiday Snaps

Poem to read when you get your photos back

Here's the beach and there's the pier.
Oh no! I think that's my left ear.

Wherever have the seagulls gone?
Did I leave the lens cap on?

Billy's playing in the sand.
No, my mistake, it's just my hand.

The baby loved the roundabout.
I rather think my film ran out.

Look, the cliffs are dazzling white—
Or was the button set on 'bright'?

My bedroom had amazing views.
I tried to film them . . . shot my shoes.

Next holiday, I think I'll find
I've left my camera behind.

Alison Chisholm

Potion for the Post-Holiday Blues

Poem to say dreamily

Though sadly the holiday may be all gone,
still slip your holiday clothes on.
Gather your photographs and cast them in a circle
  all around.
Stack your souvenirs in a mighty mound.
Bring out those things with sweet holiday smells,
then scatter an outer circle of sea shells.
Next put on a happy holiday hat
and lay out the cricket wickets, ball, and bat.
Finally close your eyes to travel to any destination—
with just a sprinkle of imagination.

Tim Pointon

Holiday Horrors

If you can't find one to fit your holiday horror,
try making up your own

Been on holiday.
Not much fun.
Burned beetroot-red:
Too much sun.

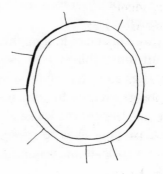

Skiing holiday.
Nasty trip.
Broke my nose,
One arm, one hip.

Camping holiday.
Won't go again.
Leaky tent.
A whole week's rain.

Italian holiday.
Robbed in Rome.
Advice to you?
Just stay at home!

Went to China.
Rotten food.
Can't tell you more:
It's far too rude!

Biking holiday
With my mum.
Too long in saddle:
Quite sore bum.

A week at sea
In hired boat.
Wobbly, sea-sick,
Bad sore throat.

Climbing holiday —
Ice and rocks.
I should have worn
Much warmer socks.

Walking holiday.
Endless heat.
Mile after mile.
Poor, blistered feet.

Hotel toilet
In a rush.
Nasty problem!
Loo won't flush!

John Kitching

Acknowledgements

Every effort has been made to trace and contact copyright holders before publication and we are grateful to all those who have granted us permission. We apologize for any inadvertent errors and will be pleased to rectify these at the earliest opportunity.

Petonelle Archer: 'Holiday Weather', copyright © Petonelle Archer 2004.
David Bateman: 'Do Have a Nice Day at the Beach', copyright © David Bateman 2004.
Gerard Benson: 'No Passport', copyright © Gerard Benson 2004.
Clare Bevan: 'Pass the Bucket', copyright © Clare Bevan 2004.
Madeleine Bingham: 'Desperation—in Eight Languages', copyright © Madeleine Bingham 2004.
Alison Chisholm: 'Air Cares' and 'Holiday Snaps', copyright © Alison Chisholm 2004.
David Clayton: 'We're Not Eating . . . ', copyright © David Clayton 2004.
Paul Cookson: 'At the Bed and Breakfast' and 'The Hunk', copyright © Paul Cookson 2004.
John C. Desmond: 'If You Go On Safari', copyright © John C. Desmond 2004.
Peter Dixon: 'Check List' and 'Take-Off', copyright © Peter Dixon 2004.
Gina Douthwaite: 'Feeling Ferry Funny', copyright © Gina Douthwaite 2004.
Eric Finney: 'What I Did in My Summer Holiday', copyright © Eric Finney 2004.
John Foster: 'Travel Books to Read on Holiday', copyright © John Foster 2004.
Pat Gadsby: 'Seeking the Elusive Trolley', copyright © Pat Gadsby 2004.
Harry Graham: 'Presence of Mind' from *Ruthless Rhymes for Heartless Homes*, published by Dover Publications, used by permission.
David Harmer: 'Turbulent Travel', copyright © David Harmer 2004.
David Horner: 'Belt Up in the Back!', copyright © David Horner 2004.
John Irwin: 'Fantastic Facts', copyright © John Irwin 2000, used by permission of the author.
Lucinda Jacob: 'On the Sunbeds', copyright © Lucinda Jacob 2004.
Beverley Johnson: 'Ouch!', copyright © Beverley Johnson 2004.
Megan de Kantzow: 'A Curse on Thieves, Especially the One Who Takes Your Mum's Handbag', copyright © Megan de Kantzow 2004.